INDEX

INTRODUCTION

This handbook has been produced to help you plan and deliver a course enabling people – old or young, fit or frail – to prepare well for their last months on this earth. Churches run baptism and marriage preparation courses, so it's in some ways a natural development to run a death preparation course. Death is, after all, part of life. Moreover for the Christian, dying and death are not the final act of the life story but a transition point in a story that continues.

Supporting people in preparing for the momentous physical, emotional, and spiritual challenge posed by dying is a high calling but is also a demanding one.
It can be hugely rewarding but also carries some risks. The advice given in this handbook is based on work that has taken place over five years: evaluating courses, delivering training to clergy and other church leaders, listening to the feedback of course facilitators and participants, and in the light of all of this refining an understanding of best practice[1]. This means that the advice has a good evidence-base so unnecessary risks should be reduced. But by its very nature engaging with mortality is an edgy undertaking (no pun intended!), and there is no such thing as a risk-free zone.

So, while this handbook is focused on the nitty-gritty of running a course, it begins by considering some of the questions that need to be considered before rushing into it:

- **Why?**

- **When?**

- **Where?**

- **Who?**

Only then does it deal with the main practical questions:

- **How?**

- **What?**

[1] Collicutt, J. (2015). *Living in the end times*: A short course addressing end of life issues for older people in an English parish church setting. *Working with Older People*, 19, 140-149; Victoria Slater & Joanna Collicutt (2018) *Living Well in the End Times* (LWET): a project to research and support churches' engagement with death and dying, *Practical Theology*, 11:2, 176-188, DOI: 10.1080/1756073X.2018.1448568

Why?

Why run a course on this topic?

You should begin by asking the question:

'Why do I want to do this?'

- *Perhaps* you've been inspired by attending a talk or workshop on preparing for death and dying.

- *Perhaps* you've been feeling frustrated that your pastoral ministry isn't quite getting to the heart of things or that it's getting stale.

- *Perhaps* you see this as a way of drawing more people into your church or conversely of reaching out in service to the wider community.

- *Perhaps* someone has simply asked you to do this.

Each of us will have our own answer to this question.

Reflecting critically on your motives will help you gauge your degree of commitment to this particular form of ministry or whether something less demanding of time, energy, and emotion would do the job. If you decide to go ahead it will help you in designing and publicising the course. It will also help you evaluate its 'success'. For example, you may find that the course didn't attract any new people to your church but that you got to know and value some of your existing congregation in a new and deeper way or made new contacts in your local community. The course would have been unsuccessful in one respect but successful in another, and your evaluation of its overall success would depend on your motives at the start.

A second rather different question is 'Why should *any* church consider doing this?' to which there is an answer that applies to us all. The certainty of the resurrection is what gives Christians our identity, and the message we proclaim and try to live out is of life in the midst of death and hope in the midst of loss. We have something significant to say on this matter. What's more, the resurrection is our 'USP'. None of the secular groups that specialize in preparing people for death, good as many of them are, can offer hope of eternal life.

Of course, we will each have our own personal take on what the words 'resurrection' and 'eternal life' mean for us. Most people who have run Well Prepared courses say they develop a deeper sense of this through honest conversations with others that involve wondering, reflecting, explaining, telling stories, and listening.

Talking with folk about our common mortality, being alongside them in the 'valley of the shadow of death' and offering a message of Christian hope is part of the calling of *all* Christians – it's not an optional extra. Clergy from many denominations make a specific promise at ordination to 'prepare the dying for their death.'[2] This has traditionally been interpreted as deathbed ministry, but we are all dying from the day we are born and we do not know when our hour will come, so it's never too early to prepare.

Perhaps the clearest finding of our research is that older people in particular are very keen – 'desperate' is perhaps not too strong a word – to talk about death and dying, both the practicalities and the spiritual aspects. Yet they all too often find that others are reluctant to have these sorts of conversations, and it's ironic that most churches don't offer this opportunity either.

Running a formal structured course is only one of several ways of doing this, and after reading the next few sections you may decide that it isn't for you at this time. But if you do go ahead with your

---

[2] www.churchofengland.org/prayer-and-worship/worship-texts-and-resources/common-worship/ministry/common-worship-ordination-services#mm013

eyes open our research suggests that this will be one of the most rewarding things you have done in ministry. Some of the potential benefits include:

- Achieving a deep sense of intimacy with course participants
- Regaining a sense of what Christian ministry and service is all about
- Having the experience of meeting a pressing human spiritual need
- Developing your pastoral skills
- Broadening your knowledge-base in this area
- Gaining confidence in talking about big theological questions
- Being held and supported by a structure that others have tried and tested
- Learning to appreciate the life wisdom and spiritual insights of course participants
- Allowing yourself to receive care from others (course participants and co-facilitator)
- Growing spiritually through articulating and owning your own authentic perspective on these issues and seeing where more work might need to be done.

When?

When should you do it?

Timing is not a trivial consideration. The New Testament makes a lot of the timing of the passion and death of Jesus (Matthew 26:18) and of the timing of his eventual return (1 Corinthians 4:5). In a similar way much of our conception of death relates to time – 'my time is running out', 'her time had come', 'his death was untimely', and so on. There is a sense in which God's time

THERE IS A SENSE IN WHICH GOD'S TIME AND OUR TIME COME TOGETHER AT THE MOMENT OF DEATH

and our time come together at the moment of death. So in deciding to prepare for this moment we are recognising that all our plans are provisional and that our time on earth is limited; we catch a glimpse of an eternal perspective.

Running a Well Prepared course also *takes* time. The material in this handbook is for a series of six 90-minute weekly meetings. On top of this there is planning time and the course facilitators need to build in additional time for emotional 'decompression'. I provided homemade cake for my course and I found that the time spent baking the cakes became quite special, allowing me to become calm and to focus, and to step into a mindset of prayerful tender care – but it added to the preparation time. (Of course it's not essential to provide homemade cakes, but our research indicates that providing a hospitable setting over which care has evidently been taken is one of the key ingredients to a successful course.) So, choose a period which is less busy than others and, if necessary, drop some of your usual commitments for a while.

You will also need to consider personal aspects of your timing. It's usually not thought wise to do this sort of work if you are recently bereaved. On the other hand, at certain periods in our lives we may be losing older relatives and friends on a fairly regular basis, so finding a bereavement-free slot may not be entirely realistic; and I found, unexpectedly, that facilitating a course helped me deal with a recent bereavement. A lot depends on how emotionally resilient you are at the time, and it is a good idea to discuss your particular situation with those who know you well.

CHOOSE A PERIOD THAT IS LESS BUSY THAN OTHERS

These principles also apply to potential course participants; certain individuals may not be in the best frame of mind to benefit from the course at a particular time, but, unlike the facilitators, they can always decide to pull out if it becomes too challenging. More widely there can be seasons in the life of a community where this seems to be just the right thing to do, and other times when it clearly is not.

The time of day and year when you hold the course will depend on the needs of your participants. In general, older people do not like to venture out on winter evenings. It has been traditional to talk about death around Remembrance Sunday and All Souls' Day, but this is just the time of year when the evenings are drawing in. What's more, it may be easier for people of all ages to approach this potentially dark and gloomy subject at a time when the days are lengthening (during Lent or after Easter) or in early autumn when nature's preparation for sleep appears so beautiful. Beauty not only gives us pleasure; it can communicate meaning and through this instil peace.

Where?

Where should you hold it?

The key aspects of your chosen environment are that it should feel safe and hospitable.

There are pros and cons to running a course in a church. The pros are that churches are often beautiful spaces that encourage reflection; older churches will be full of reminders both that we die but also that we can leave a legacy of memories behind us; access to a pleasant churchyard can be even more helpful[3], and, if the weather permits, you might hold one or more sessions outside. On the other hand churches can feel creepy and can be a place of bad memories for some; it may be difficult for people to connect what is said in this special environment with their ordinary daily lives; churches are not always physically accessible or comfortable.

THE KEY ASPECTS OF YOUR CHOSEN ENVIRONMENT ARE THAT IT SHOULD FEEL SAFE AND HOSPITABLE.

Running a course in someone's home has the advantage of providing a feeling of hospitable domesticity, but it is probably not a good idea. The space is too personal for someone to get up and leave without appearing rude. It can be difficult to voice disagreement with someone if you are in their home. The room in which feelings of grief or fear have been expressed may become a difficult place for the host to feel relaxed after the participants have departed.

[3] For more ideas on making the most of churchyards see www.caringforgodsacre.org.uk

So, ideally the course should be held in a more neutral space such as a church room or a community facility, which has good access and, ideally, with a loop system in place. You will need facilities for making a hot drink, and toilets. It's important that participants can see out and feel they can get out easily. A café style arrangement works well, but it may on occasion be good to arrange chairs in a horseshoe facing a window (especially if the view is pleasant and restful or busy and full of 'normal' life). This dilutes the intensity of the experience, gives a broader perspective, and allows participants to 'zone out' as necessary and spend time with their own thoughts.

A further option is to run a bespoke group in a residential home or sheltered housing setting. Again, choosing a safe, hospitable, private, and neutral space within this setting will be an important part of your planning.

Who?

Who is the course for?

You will need to decide whether the course is run as part of the programme of an existing group whose members already know each other (for example a Mothers' Union, a carers' support group, or residents in a care home) or whether it is a stand-alone event. You may want to offer it for all ages of adult or target a specific age group. You may want to run an ecumenical group or to open it to people in your locality of all faiths and none. Your decision on this will affect the content of your sessions (though perhaps not as much as you might think). It will also affect the way you contact potential participants. It's wise to have an upper limit on group size; 12-15 participants is a reasonable maximum.

THESE COURSES ARE COMMUNITIES OF MUTUAL LEARNING IN WHICH THE FACILITATORS MAY GAIN AS MUCH AS THE PARTICIPANTS.

These courses are communities of mutual learning in which the facilitators may gain as much as the participants. One course facilitator who kept a journal to record her experiences said: "I'm on the same journey…. it's not just me leading a group of others but the same issues that I am inviting them to engage with I engage with myself."

Who will run the course?

You will need help and support in running a course; there should be at least two facilitators for each session. If there are two facilitators

YOU MAY NOT HAVE ALL THE 'HEAD' ANSWERS BUT YOU DO NEED TO HAVE HEART-FELT ASSURANCE.

one person can be giving the main input while the other is on hand to deal with practical issues or to attend to anyone who becomes distressed or is in danger of dominating discussions. This is all part of sensitive handling of group dynamics, so that one person doesn't take over the whole session and impose their agenda on it, and the more reticent members of the group can be drawn out.

The facilitators can support each other and offer constructive feedback. Recall that Jesus sent out disciples in pairs (Luke 10:1). Our research also indicates that there should be continuity, so at least one of the facilitators should be there throughout the course even if you invite guest speakers for certain sessions.

The facilitators do not need to have all the practical and theological answers about death and dying. Instead you need to be prepared by having reflected honestly and prayerfully about your attitude to and experience of this area. There are some exercises on pages 34–35 to help you do this. You also need to have some experience of being alongside people who are questioning, confused, or in distress, to be prepared to listen openly to them, to tolerate uncertainty, and to be

OK with acknowledging mystery and admitting that you don't know.

But you also need to have a clear sense of the basis of your hope so that you can communicate this feeling to others with a sense of authenticity. You may not have all the 'head' answers but you do need to have heart-felt assurance. This will not be based so much on the sort of theology to be found in the creeds or academic textbooks but more on your lived experience of God, and it might be felt as inner convictions rather like these:

- God is love and wants to give us our hearts' desire.
- God is with us and will never let us go.
- God is fair – not moody or cruel – and knows each person's back-story
- The facts are friendly (because in Jesus God acted decisively to redeem this broken world)
- The human body is precious and important (because Jesus' body was precious and important – even after death)

Convictions like these don't necessarily have to be spelt out to others (though you may find yourself expressing them on occasion). It's more that these will be the foundation on which everything you say and do rests, and will be picked up intuitively by the participants.

How?

How should it be run?

Death is frightening, in both its physical and existential aspects. Here are just some of the things that make it so deeply challenging:

- It is fundamentally uncontrollable and unpredictable
- It involves (unknown and possibly extreme) degrees of physical pain and discomfort
- It separates loved-ones
- It is undergone alone
- It interrupts our plans and projects, and may make life seem pointless
- It seems to annihilate those who undergo it
- It comes to us all

It was Sigmund Freud who first pointed out that we deal with frightening stuff by pushing it right to the back of our minds. We do this both as individuals and as a society. In twenty-first century Britain the process of caring for the dying and managing death has been largely handed over to professionals. This means that we can avoid engaging with it until a close loved-one dies, and for many of us this does not happen until middle age. Indeed it is possible for us to go through our whole life without ever having seen the body of a person who has died.

So, inviting people to talk about death is inviting them to do something that may well break the habits of a lifetime; it will involve stepping into unknown and possibly scary territory. This means that the facilitators need to lead the participants into this place with a mix of gentleness and confidence, a step at a time. Psalm 23 talks of the comfort provided by the LORD's rod and staff as the psalmist walks through the valley of the shadow of death. This comfort can be provided by two things – the way the course is structured and the provision of a 'holding environment' by the facilitators. Ways of doing this are explored in the next two sections.

How to structure the course

Imagine that you are exploring the ocean with some novice divers. The movement is down and away from the light, noise, and fresh air of everyday life into a place that is dark and disorienting but full of treasures, followed by a gradual return to normality. You need a good oxygen supply yourself (hence the need for personal preparation), and you need to be able to signal clearly to your pupils to indicate where they are, what is happening, and whether or not things are OK. Each session may take them a little deeper, but they always return to the light. Running a Well Prepared course is very like this.

Each session of the course should have the same structure, almost like a ritual. You will need to signal the beginning and the end clearly. One way of signalling the end of the session is to say the same prayer every time; this reminds the participants that we are all in God's hands and is a calming way to give closure. If your group consists of people from different faith backgrounds a good prayer to use is based Number 6:24-26:

> The LORD [or God] bless you and keep you;
> the LORD [or God] make his face to shine upon you,
> and be gracious to you;
> the LORD [or God] lift up his countenance upon you,
> and give you peace.

As already noted, it is important to offer time and space for decompression – a kind of buffer zone between the emotionally significant material and mundane life. Half an hour for sharing tea and cake after an hour's session is ideal.

Just as each session can be thought of as a journey into the deep and back again, so can the whole course. This is why the most emotionally challenging material (the physical reality of death) is best dealt with in the middle of the course, led into gradually via practical sessions and followed by more emotionally comforting content. You should give some attention to the way that you end the whole course and the process of parting.

The whole journey must feel as safe as possible. This can be helped a lot by providing good information – a flyer (see page 73) setting out clearly what participants can expect and a verbal summary at the beginning of each session; people shouldn't be taken by surprise. It is also important to set some confidentiality boundaries such as 'Chatham House rules'; people need to know that what they have shared remains within the group[4].

THE WHOLE JOURNEY MUST FEEL AS SAFE AS POSSIBLE.

You should give some thought to follow-up. If participants have continuing needs or questions that have been opened up by attending the course is there someone you can point them to after it has finished so that they are not left unsupported? In the case where you are pastorally responsible for some or all of the participants, follow-up may involve a personal visit, encouraging participants to continue to meet on their own, recommending some further reading, or it may mean planning another event in your

[4] The exception to this is if a participant discloses a safeguarding related issue. In this case you should seek advice from your church safeguarding officer, or if that is not possible, from your local adult safeguarding board. www.scie.org.uk/care-act-2014/safeguarding-adults/safeguarding-adults-boards-checklist-and-resources/role-and-duties.asp

church such as a service of remembrance, a quiet day, or a series of sermons. Be realistic about what you can offer within the resources available to you.

How to provide a 'holding environment'

When working pastorally with people who are engaging with the prospect of their own death you will need to give out signals that they will be 'held' as they experience and struggle with distressing feelings. You will not rub their noses in these feelings, but will instead support them in regulating *themselves* as they establish their own balance between raw emotion and coping strategies such as humour and practical chat. You will need to go with their flow.

> **YOU WILL NEED TO GIVE OUT SIGNALS THAT THEY WILL BE 'HELD' AS THEY EXPERIENCE AND STRUGGLE WITH DISTRESSING FEELINGS.**

If someone wants to leave the group for a few minutes, or to go home, or to miss a session because the topic seems too challenging, that is fine; they are simply taking responsibility for managing their own emotions. If someone becomes quietly distressed in a group session but does not choose to leave that is fine also; here you need to keep the tone relaxed and unfussy, showing that it is OK – in fact normal – to express emotion in these circumstances.

Having a box of tissues to hand is always useful, but remember that tears are not the only way that people express distress; be attentive to people's facial expressions and body language.

It's worth being aware of two natural healing processes that can be harnessed as part of providing a holding environment. The first is called 'reciprocal inhibition'. This is where two activities work against each other: we cannot eat or play when we are afraid and conversely nice food and a playful ambience both reduce fear. As someone once put it, 'If you're eating cake you know you're not dead.' Our research findings showed that course participants really appreciated humour and laughter, which, much to their surprise, transformed an experience that could have been very gloomy into fun.

IF YOU'RE EATING CAKE YOU KNOW YOU'RE NOT DEAD

The second healing process is called 'habituation'. This is grounded in our biology. It describes the almost universal experience that when we confront the thing that we have been avoiding it can be very unpleasant at first, but our initial discomfort will decrease to manageable levels fairly quickly. If we stick with it we will go on to experience a sense of mastery and achievement, so that the next encounter is much less difficult and our confidence builds. Trusting this process of habituation to do its work by keeping a calm demeanour and communicating a sense that all will be well is part of what it means to provide a holding environment.

How to support participants in their learning

The need to be pastorally sensitive should not mislead you into thinking of the sessions as 'therapy'. This is a course in which participants will be reflecting and learning, not a therapy programme. So, providing a holding environment is not an end in itself but a starting point for learning.

IT PAYS TO HAVE SEVERAL FLEXIBLE MODES OF DELIVERY TO SUIT THE INDIVIDUAL(S) AND THE SITUATION.

Different people have different preferred learning styles. They also have different learning histories. Some will have really enjoyed school; others may associate school with bullying, humiliation and failure. Some respond well to group discussion; others want to be talked at. Some love music and the visual arts; they leave others cold. Some like the worldwide web; others (especially older people or those on low incomes) find it difficult to access. Some want to plumb emotional and spiritual depths; others want to dip their toe in the water. When trying to facilitate exploration of death and dying it pays to have several flexible modes of delivery to suit the individual(s) and the situation.

In our research we found that the favourite sessions for some were the least liked by others. The differences in preference may have been down to personality, but in one group at least, it also seemed to relate to gender, with the men preferring a robust approach and the women preferring something gentler and more subtle. This may not be true across the board, but it is worth paying attention to gender balance (and other factors of culture and ethnicity) when thinking about facilitators or guest speakers.

Giving the participants activities to do between sessions will help them to carry their learning over into the rest of their lives, engage with the material in greater depth, and take responsibility for their own learning. I discovered the hard way that it is not a good idea to refer to these activities as 'homework', as this term has negative connotations for many people.

What?

What resources need to be in place before you begin?

> *"Suddenly I realized – two people isn't enough. You need backup. If there are only two people, and someone drops off the edge, then you're on your own. Two isn't a large enough number. You need three at least* [5]. *"*

Even though at least two of you will be involved in facilitating the course, it's important to have some further support, specifically in the areas of prayer and supervision. It's good to ask for this work to be remembered as part of regular church services or pastoral team meetings, but you may also want to set up a small group who will specifically pray for this project either as a virtual network or by meeting together.

It's also advisable to make contact with someone who has expertise in the area of death and dying, perhaps a health care professional or hospital or hospice chaplain, who is willing to be available at the end of a phone in case you run into unexpected difficulties.

It's likely you will want to invite some additional speakers for certain sessions, for example a palliative care practitioner, a funeral director, or a solicitor. Make contact with them well in advance to ensure that you can get to know them a little and so that they will have a clear understanding of what you are asking them to do. It's usually advisable to put this in writing; it's easy for busy people to forget the precise details of what's required for a particular occasion and then just revert to their usual spiel, which may not fit the bill for your specific situation.

[5] About a boy (2002), Screenplay Chris Weitz, Paul Weitz, Peter Hedges

If you're planning to play music (which is almost certain) make sure you have equipment that will work in your chosen venue. If you're planning some artwork, you'll need to budget for and obtain some materials. It's important that these are new rather than stuff you have left over in the cupboard.

There's a lot of free published material available, and it's being updated all the time. As many older people do not have ready access to the internet it's a good idea to download or send off in advance for printed versions of the literature you may want to use. Go to **www.deathlife.org.uk/good-practice/help/** for details of organisations you should consult.

What are the underlying themes of the whole course?

The sessions should include material on:

- Looking back and letting go
- Savouring life now
- Looking forward in hope

Looking back

Preparing well for death involves a delicate balance between staying in control and letting go. This balance is something that we all struggle with, and it will change depending on where we are on our 'death trajectory'. Your course should raise early on the prospect of beginning to let go of things in this life. The most concrete way of doing this is deciding to make a will, but there are other ways of 'putting one's affairs in order.' These include drawing the various threads of one's life together to weave a coherent story, and also dealing with unfinished business (be it pleasant or painful) in relationships.

Just as we are usually advised to update our wills every ten years, we also need to do some regular updating of the story of our lives. For a younger person it may feel as if there are many chapters left to come. Surprisingly, this may also be true for an older person, especially if he or she believes that life continues after death. For other older or terminally ill people there is a real sense that the story is moving to a close; one older person whispered to me hours before his death, 'And we all lived happily ever after.' He had literally completed the story of his (earthly) life.

PREPARING WELL FOR DEATH INVOLVES A DELICATE BALANCE BETWEEN STAYING IN CONTROL AND LETTING GO.

Savouring life

But we should live fully until we die. So it's important to support people in inhabiting the present with gratitude and with a sense that they can continue to grow as human beings right up to the end of their lives. There are practical and active ways to do this, but it can also be about reframing the way we see things. For example, very old or chronically sick people can feel as if they are just marking time in a waiting room, yet this period of life can yield unforeseen treasures. Bodily losses and hardship, painful as they undoubtedly are, can make people spiritually more aware as they focus on the essentials of life. And as this life draws towards its end there can be a sense of standing poised at the threshold of something new; for some this feels so real that they can almost see and touch it. It's as if a spiritual mountaintop has been reached that offers vistas unseen by most people. This gives a whole new meaning to the phrase 'Over the hill'. It affirms the value of people – young or old – who are in their last years, months, or days as people of special wisdom and insight.

If your group is made up of frail or very old people you might like to explore this idea with them, helping them to value and voice their experiences.

Looking forward

Planning for a time when one no longer has capacity to make decisions (usually done through a Lasting Power of Attorney) is wise, and your course can draw this to people's attention and show them how to take the first steps. Planning one's funeral both helps in the process of facing up to what is coming and (if not over-prescriptive) can be a gift to those left behind.

OUR RESEARCH HAS FOUND THAT PEOPLE ARE EAGER TO TALK ABOUT WHAT HAPPENS AFTER DEATH.

While death is ultimately uncontrollable, we are fortunate in this country to have the right to make informed choices about our dying. However, our reticence in talking about death can make this a daunting prospect. Your course can begin to open up conversations about the options available and how to communicate personal wishes to medical staff and loved ones. These conversations should not just be about physical and social care but also about spiritual care.

Finally, our research has found that people are eager to talk about what happens after death. They have many questions, hopes, and fears. Even if they have been faithful Christians for many years their thoughts will not always fit neatly into textbook Christian theology, but they should not be dismissed for that. Helping people to explore their ideas about life and death and to make connections with the Christian story is one of the most exciting aspects of running this sort of course.

PREPARE YOURSELF

Before leading a Well Prepared course, do the following exercises. They should help put you in touch with some of your own feelings about death and dying.

1 Remember a time

This should take about 10 minutes but you should allow some time before to find a quiet place where you won't be disturbed and to be still. You will need to allow some time afterwards to come back into the land of the living.

Recall a memorable experience that you have had in relation to death and dying. Choose a specific event that lasted from a few moments up to a few hours, not a general set of experiences.

Write about this as if you were talking to a good friend. Describe what happened, when and where it happened, and what you were thinking and feeling at the time. You may also want to add some reflections that emerged afterwards.

2

Be aware of your attitude towards death

Go to the Course page of the Death and Life website (www.deathlife.org.uk/course/). There you find a questionnaire that you can download. The questionnaire is a version of a research tool called the 'Death Attitudes Profile- Revised'. It consists of a number of statements related to different attitudes towards death. The overall score isn't important, but filling in the questionnaire should make you more aware of your attitude to death. Read each statement carefully and then indicate the extent to which you agree or disagree by circling the appropriate statement.

3

Reflect on a Bible passage

Choose a phrase or verse from the Bible that sums up your hope in the face of death, for example 'with the Lord forever', 'life in its fullness', 'then we will see face to face', 'do not be afraid: you are worth more than many sparrows'. Reflect prayerfully on why it is precious to you.

THE SESSIONS

SESSION 1
BE PREPARED

Welcome and introduction

15 MINS

Begin the session by introducing yourself and offering words of welcome. Explain what the course is about. It's helpful to have this written down. On page 73, you can find a link to the website resources, including a flyer which also explains what the course is about.

It may also be helpful to begin by reading a poem. Choose one suitable to your participants and avoid highly religious or sentimental poems. The idea is simply to get the subject on the table, not to communicate deep truths or religious dogma.

We have used *The gifts of death* by Connie Barlow[6] and Joan Walsh Anglund's very brief poem, 'The miracle is that life continues. The sorrow is that we do not.'[7]

In their different ways these communicate the reality of death but also frame it as something natural, and they contain within them seeds of hope.

Invite any initial reflections on the poem but do not offer your own.

Explain that the focus on this first session is looking forward and preparing. For older generations prudence was seen as a virtue; being well prepared for future eventualities is easily recognised as wise by people over 60. This is not so much the case with younger people and may need more in the way of discussion.

---

[6] www.huffingtonpost.com/rev-michael-dowd/a-scientific-honoring-of-death_b_1556839.html

[7] A slice of snow (1970), London: Collins, p. 15.

Making a will and LPA

40 MINS

Have a short presentation on making a will and invite participants to ask questions or share experiences. Remind participants that 'You can't take it with you', and introduce the idea of letting go well. Reflect on the way that people can dispose of their worldly goods in a way that ensures peace between those left behind or, on the other hand, sows discord and conflict that may persist for generations. It's likely that some of your participants will have first-hand experience of this that they may wish to share this. Address the tricky issue of who to choose as executor; make it clear that this doesn't have to be a family member, and indeed it can be helpful to have an executor who has a bit of emotional distance. This can be a liberating discovery for some people who are caught up in unhelpful family dynamics. The executor needs to be named in the will, and when it is finally signed this must be witnessed by two people who are not beneficiaries and who also need to sign it. It is advisable (though not legally required) to have help from a solicitor when making a will.

Most people are reasonably familiar with the process of making a will but 'Lasting Power of Attorney' (LPA) may need more in the way of explanation. An LPA is a document in which you authorise two or more named individuals to act in your interests in the event that you become 'incapable'[8]. The individuals acting for you are called 'attorneys'. You can make an LPA for decisions about your property and finances OR about your health and general welfare. It's advisable for LPAs to be drawn up by a solicitor, but you can do it yourself online[9]. It needs to be registered with the Public Guardian

[8] This is a technical use of the word as found in the Mental Capacity Act of 2005.
www.nhs.uk/Conditions/social-care-and-support-guide/Pages/mental-capacity.aspx

[9] www.lastingpowerofattorney.service.gov.uk/home

and this will involve paying a fee [10].

It's desirable that this presentation on wills and LPAs is given by an invited expert. Whether you use an expert or try and do it yourself you should make sure that you have up to date accessible literature on these topics available for your participants to take away. The Law Society, Age UK, and the Alzheimer's Society are the best sources.

Conclusion

Introduce participants to the idea of carrying out an activity in preparation for the next session. In order to transition from the idea of letting go of possessions into the area of life stories, invite participants to consider two questions:

5 MINS

1. How would you like to be remembered by people after
you have died?

2. What gem of wisdom would you like to pass on to those left behind?

Finish with a prayer, if appropriate.

[10] www.gov.uk/government/organisations/office-of-the-public-guardian

SESSION 2
THE STORY OF MY LIFE

Welcome

Begin the session by welcoming any newcomers and briefly reminding participants of what was covered in the previous session.

2-3 MINS Move into the topic by suggesting that part of living well in our last days is to go about the task of drawing all the threads of our life story together, to reflect on what it was all about and, from the perspective of a whole life lived, to ask again the question, 'Who am I?'

Identity discussion

Remind the participants of the questions they were asked to consider at the end of the previous session (it may help to have these written out on a flip chart). Depending on the size of your group you may want

20 MINS to ask participants to break into smaller groups of about half a dozen to discuss the first question. After 10 minutes or so reconvene to gather responses; then repeat the procedure for the second question.

Creative response

There are various ways of working creatively with the themes that emerge:

30 MINS

- Making a wisdom tree, using a branch as a framework and tying paper leaves with participants' responses written on them. This would make a good prayer installation for a church or a school.

Writing a 'gratitude' letter to someone who has made a difference in participants' lives but whom they have never had a chance to thank. Knowing you have made a difference is one of the things that gives people satisfaction at the end of life. The letter might be posted or simply written and kept (and this will clearly be necessary if the individual concerned has already died). It could form a focus for personal prayer. You might provide 'Thank you' cards for this purpose. Consider a similar exercise with 'Sorry' cards; this would obviously be more emotionally demanding and is probably best offered as an exercise participants might pursue in their own time.

Inviting participants to write an epitaph or create a design for their headstone. In 2017 the artist Alan Kane invited ten young people between the ages of 15 and 18 to develop proposals for their own headstones. They responded thoughtfully and playfully, producing poignant and often humorous designs. The result was the 'Early Graves' exhibition [11] at the Royal Shakespeare Company in Stratford-upon-Avon.

Making memory boxes (see facing page). You could either share memory boxes made by the facilitators as examples, or the previous week you could have asked participants to bring one item that they would like to put in a memory box and invite them to speak about this. There will not be time for every participant to make and share a whole memory box in the session, but you should consider this as a separate activity, perhaps as a follow up to your group. It is an ideal activity for adults and children to do together.

---

[11] cdn2.rsc.org.uk/sitefinity/exhibitions-pdfs/b7872_1early_graves_accessible_guide-(002).pdf?sfvrsn=0

66 The box should be large enough to accommodate several items but not too large to carry around. A large shoe box is about the right size. The box can be covered in a decoration that expresses something about those making it. The contents should be a variety of objects that signify important parts of the life of the individual or community. It is useful to include a short written explanation of the items…

My experience of sharing memory boxes in a group is that we quickly establish intimacy with each other. People who think they know each other well are surprised to find out new and significant things about their companions…

Memory boxes can also be a precious legacy for those left behind…The box can give a sense of what 'Grandma was really like.' I know one woman in her fifties who insisted on including a pair of black silk stockings in her memory box. This was so that any future grandchildren who knew her only as frail and forgetful would understand that she had in earlier days been a vibrant, sexy, and sensual woman, and that this was also part of her story. 99

From *Thinking of You* by Joanna Collicutt [12]

[12] Collicutt, J. (2017). *Thinking of you: A resource for the spiritual care of people with dementia.* Oxford: BRF, pp.133-34.

Reflection on the session

5 MINS

Before you finish the session make sure you devote a few minutes to drawing out some themes and reflecting on them. Try and turn the session itself into a story by summarising what was done and said. One helpful image of living life well is that of weaving a tapestry out of many different threads, so that they are not tangled or left hanging but come together in a unique and beautiful way. This weaving should go on throughout our life, but in its final years it naturally becomes more intense. This is an image that works particularly well in my community of Witney whose identity is strongly connected with blanket-weaving. You may find that you are able to come up with an image that makes special sense in your own setting.

Depending on the faith and personalities of your participants, you may wish to bring this natural image into conversation with the Christian story. You might ask if God is part of the story or tapestry and, if so, how? You might want to speak of God knowing our whole story (Psalm 139), calling us by name (Isaiah 43:1-3) or knowing us as unique individuals (Isaiah 49:15-16). Make sure this part of the session stays more like a conversation than a sermon.

Conclusion

Finally invite participants to carry out two activities, both linking the idea of identity with the funeral, in preparation for the next session:

2-3 MINS

1. Bring a reading that you would like at your funeral

2. Think about this question: 'Who is my funeral for?'

Finish with a prayer, if appropriate.

SESSION 3
PLANNING MY FUNERAL

Welcome

2-3 MINS Begin the session by welcoming any newcomers (this is probably the latest point at which people could join the course) and briefly reminding participants of what was covered in the previous session. Try and link the idea of identity with the task of planning one's funeral, and also loop back to the idea of balancing letting go with being in control.

What (and who) is a funeral for?

10 MINS It's helpful for participants to think about whether the funeral is primarily a means of asserting their identity – 'This was/is me!' – or whether it's really to help those left behind to say goodbye, or whether it is something else altogether – a handing over of the deceased into the care of God. Perhaps it's all of these, and they need to be held together.

Choosing hymns and poems

20 MINS Divide into smaller groups of three or so and ask participants to share their choices of funeral poems with each other. If some have not brought poems they could talk about a favourite hymn (it's helpful to have hymn books to hand), or you may wish to provide some copies of poems that are often used for funerals. These are readily available on the internet. Good published resources include 'Heaven's morning breaks' by Jeremy Brooks, 'Readings for funerals' by Mark Oakley, and 'Poems and readings for funerals' by Julia Watson[13]. Devote about 20 minutes to this activity.

[13] Brooks, J. (2013). *Heaven's morning breaks: Sensitive and practical reflections on funeral practice.* Stowmarket: Kevin Mayhew; Oakley, M. (2015). *Readings for funerals.* London: SPCK: Watson, J. (2004). *Poems and readings for funerals.* London: Penguin.

Funeral practicalities

25 MINS

You may then wish to have a funeral director to give a Q & A session about current options for funerals, including pre-paid financial packages. Alternatively you may choose to talk people through the funeral service for your denomination yourself, especially if you're very experienced in taking funerals, and simply give participants written resources from a range of funeral providers.

Conclusion

2-3 MINS

Explain clearly that the next session will be on the actual process of dying, and invite participants between now and then to reflect on the question 'What is a good death?'

Finish with a prayer, if appropriate.

SESSION 4
THE LAST DAYS

Welcome and setting the scene

5 MINS

Begin the session by briefly reminding participants of what was covered in the previous session, again stressing the tension between being in control and letting go. Explain that this session will be on the actual process of dying. Depending on the make-up of your group, you may wish to read:

> 66 *In the last days it will be, God declares, that I will pour out my Spirit upon all flesh, and your sons and your daughters shall prophesy, and your young men shall see visions, and your old men shall dream dreams.* 99
> **Joel 2:28/Acts 2:17**

This reading is a way of offering the idea that the end of earthly life can be seen as a place of spiritual blessing. Nevertheless, dying is physically rigorous, and if this session is to explore it well its raw physicality must be acknowledged. Providing a holding environment will be particularly important in this session.

Next, move into the subject of the session by saying that as death approaches we move from a natural feeling of wanting to be in control of things to a readiness to let go. Of course, we are right to wish for good control of any pain and discomfort, and to be in a safe and secure place with loved ones close at hand. Today, more than ever, there's a very good chance that this is indeed what we will experience. Palliative care practice has come on in leaps and bounds in recent years, and patients now have a good deal of choice and control over where they end their days and what sort of treatment and care they wish to have. This is all part of 'a good death.'

Q&A session with palliative care professional

25 MINS

For this session it's wise to have an invited speaker who is a palliative care expert and who knows the services in your locality. Ask him or her to talk about choices for where to spend one's final days (at home, in a hospice, or a community hospital etc.), options for medical treatment at this time, how to make things as pleasant as possible, and accessing spiritual care. Much of this will be specific to your local area. If the group feels a safe enough space participants may feel emboldened to ask questions about the process of dying itself and what it might feel like. This may be a particular issue for participants who have witnessed the death of a loved-one that has not appeared peaceful.

Living wills

25 MINS

As part of this session you should discuss Advance Decisions (essentially 'living wills'). In an Advance Decision the individual sets out his or her wishes in the event that s/he becomes incapacitated and unable to communicate them directly. These wishes are usually related to medical interventions during the last days that may prolong life but not increase its quality, for example aggressive resuscitation after cardiac arrest; feeding through a tube when the individual is unconscious; giving antibiotics for pneumonia. It can also include wishes on organ donation after death.

Advance Decisions are explained on the NHS website. **www.nhs. uk/Planners/end-of-life-care/Pages/advance-decision-to-refuse-treatment.aspx** It's advisable to talk to one's GP about the process of making an Advance Decision*, and several organisations (most notably 'Compassion in Dying' produce forms and guidance). The written record can be placed in the individual's medical notes, but copies can also be made available to loved-ones. There's a UK-wide scheme (probably taken up more in some parts of the country than others) called 'Message in a Bottle' in which the individual's wishes are placed in an easily identifiable container kept in the fridge. This scheme is organised by the Lions' Clubs. For more information see: lionsclubs.co/MemberArea/?p=314.

Formal Advance Decisions* are only a part of the more general process of Advance Care Planning, in which the individual thinks through and discusses his or her wishes relating to the end of life with loved-ones and health and social care professionals (for example care of any pets that may outlive them). It may well be appropriate for a faith practitioner such as a vicar or chaplain to be part of this process, so that spiritual needs at the time of death are not forgotten. An example of the sort of thing that might be included would be, 'If I am found unconscious please call my parish priest on this number…' (You should provide an opportunity to go into spiritual care around the time of death in more detail in the next session, but flag it up here.)

As the discussion draws to a close you may wish to reflect on the idea that dying is in many ways like giving birth. It's wise and reassuring to have a birth plan, but sometimes events take over and labour is not fully controllable. It is also wise and reassuring to have a death plan, but at the end of the day we should acknowledge that death is not fully controllable either.

> *** NB Advance Decisions are NOT 'assisted dying'.** It is very important that participants understand that making an Advance Decision is not the same as requesting 'assisted dying', which is*

currently illegal in the UK[14]. *This may be an area of confusion for participants, not helped by the fact that the two key campaign groups on the two questions have similar names ('Compassion in Dying' for Advance Decisions, and 'Dignity in Dying' for assisted dying).*

You may find that some of your group are keen to discuss issues around assisted dying further. This should not distract from the main focus of the session, so it may be necessary for you to arrange a separate event to enable this to happen. If you do this it will be helpful to consult a web-based resource recently constructed by the University of Cardiff called 'Christian perspectives on death and dying'. It covers both Advance Decisions and assisted dying: xerte.cardiff.ac.uk/play_5767

There are profound disagreements about this issue both within the church and in wider society. The theological arguments against it rest on the idea that life is a gift from God (Genesis 2:7) and that only God can take it back through natural processes, it is not ours to give back. The theological arguments in favour of it rest on the idea that God is compassionate and is not in the business of burdening his people (Luke 11:46; Matthew 11:28-30). An open attitude to the issue is pastorally appropriate, even if you have strong personal views. If a vulnerable person raises this question, it is wise to probe further, as there may be safeguarding implications.

[14] See, for example The Commission for Assisted Dying, (2012). 'The current status of assisted dying is inadequate and incoherent…' (London: Demos) www.demos.co.uk/files/476_CoAD_FinalReport_158x240_1_web_single-NEW_.pdf?1328113363

Conclusion

5 MINS

Invite participants to prepare for the next session which will be entitled 'Departing in peace'. (It's a good idea to mention the word 'peace' at this point as it will signal the move from talking about potentially disturbing issues to a place of relative calm.) There are two possible activities for the next session, and which you choose will depend on the nature of your group. The first option is to share participants' choices of music to 'go out to' – what they would like to hear in their final days and hours. In this case invite participants to bring the music with them (or at least to let you know in advance so that you can try and source it). The second is to have a 'bucket list' discussion; what things do they feel they need to have done in order to depart in peace? In this case invite participants to come with ideas and stories appropriate to the task.

Finish with a prayer, if appropriate.

SESSION 5
DEPARTING IN PEACE

Welcome and setting the scene

15 MINS

Begin the session by briefly reminding participants of what was covered in the previous session, making the link between a good death and departing in peace. Read Simeon's song:

> *Lord, now lettest thou thy servant depart in peace according to thy word. For mine eyes have seen thy salvation, which thou hast prepared before the face of all people; to be a light to lighten the Gentiles and to be the glory of thy people Israel.*
> Luke 2:29-32 (BCP)

Reflect on the fact that Simeon had a strong sense of what he would need to have seen and done in order to depart in peace. Note that this was not primarily about looking back or about thinking about himself, but about looking to the future and the needs of others – in fact the whole world. Simeon is seeing deep meaning and purpose in things, and so he can leave this life content. Note also that we are not told what age Simeon was; it's possible that he was a young or middle-aged man, so his song can apply to people of all ages facing death.

To set the scene further, you may wish to play all or part of the very beautiful aria *Schlummert ein, ihr matten Augen* ('Rest weary eyes') from J.S. Bach's setting of Simeon's song, *Ich Habe Genug* ('I have enough') BWV 82: **www.youtube.com/watch?v=QioNzrN9wdI**

Spiritual care at the time of death

15 MINS

Talk to participants about what the Christian Church offers in the last days. If some of your participants are of other faith traditions it will be important to acknowledge this and point them in the direction of someone to talk to from their own tradition, but they may still be interested in what Christians do; you should not be ashamed of the clearly faith-based aspect of the course. In the Church of England, this is set out in the Common Worship Pastoral Services book section 'Ministry at the time of death' [15]. You may want to have some copies of the prayers, particularly those for 'Laying on of Hands and Anointing' and 'Commendation' available for participants to read and take away (or the equivalent from your own denomination). These are deeply comforting and go some way to dispelling anxieties evoked by terms such as 'Last rites' and 'Extreme Unction'.

At this point you may wish to draw any local volunteer end of life befriending schemes to the attention of your participants. (The availability of these varies across the country and you will need to do some of your own research into this. Contacting your local hospice is a good place to start).

[15] The Archbishops' Council (2000). Common Worship Pastoral Services (London: Church House Publishing), pp. 216-35. www.churchofengland.org/prayer-and-worship/worship-texts-and-resources/common-worship/death-and-dying/funeral#mm112

Bucket-list or 'music to go out to'

25 MINS

In both of these you will need to allow those participants who wish to, to tell something of their own story without one person dominating the group. You will also need to draw out some common themes as you sum up the session. For example, when I facilitated one 'music to go out to' session I noticed that several of the chosen pieces were like lullabies (as is *Schlummer ein*), some evoked childhood memories, and some soared high, evoking bird flight. This led to a brief reflection on dying as being respectively like going to sleep, like going home at last, and a liberation of the human spirit.

Conclusion

2-3 MINS

Invite participants to prepare for the next session by considering the question of what happens after we die (if anything).

Finish with a prayer, if appropriate.

SESSION 6
WHAT COMES NEXT?

Welcome

5 MINS

Begin by saying that the question mark in the title of this session is important. None of us has gone through death and come out the other side, so all our statements about it are conjecture, some more informed than others. The Bible itself speaks with many voices on this issue. The New Testament is based on a rock-solid belief in the raising of Christ; it nevertheless offers a multifaceted account made up of many separate images, none of which does full justice to the reality of the resurrection life. This remains deeply mysterious territory.

Creative activities and reflection

40 MINS

This session aims to give participants permission to advance tentative, provisional ideas and images, hopes and fears, rather than giving them all the answers. You might think of this as hearing their stories so that you can bring these into conversation with God's story. There are a number of ways of doing this and you should be guided by the needs of your particular group.

You could use various forms of visual art media – collage, paints, pastels etc; alongside this you might also offer participants the opportunity to write poetry (what one person referred to as 'my painting in words'). Another way is to engage with the Death and Life reflection cards that can be bought at **https://store.oxford.anglican. org/products/deathlife-cards/**. These place biblical themes alongside a variety of images to encourage individual reflection or discussion in small groups of two or three.

The session should have an even balance between creative or reflective activity and input from the facilitator(s). Your input should be to explore questions raised, affirm the ideas and images generated and link them with aspects of the Christian tradition.

Facilitating reflection

The way human beings think about death seems to be marked by a number of recurring themes. Some of these are therefore likely to come up in the activity and discussion. Some may have come up already in earlier sessions, and so you may be able to make helpful links back across the whole course:

- Dying as a kind of labour, and therefore death as a kind of rebirth
- Death as a final, well deserved, peaceful sleep
- Death as going home
- Death as the next phase in the deceased's journey: a pilgrimage, a heroic quest, another chance to right wrongs
- Death as a return to the place from where the deceased first came: the stars, the earth, parents or ancestors
- Death as liberation from captivity

We find such metaphors – commonly expressed in poetry, music, and images from nature such as clouds, the greening of spring, or the flight of winged creatures – plausible even in the face of the self-evident bodily decay of the deceased. Part of the human process of grief seems to involve an attunement to the presence of the deceased in certain natural forms and creatures.

A moving example of this sort of instinct at work is given by the writer Paul Heiney in account of his sea voyages in the period following the loss of his son, Nicholas, at the age of 23:

> **❝** *Sailing out from Mar del Plata three days later, a snowy white bird — possibly a tern — circled overhead. I watched it power through the disturbed air in the lee of the mainsail before soaring high, then swooping, almost to land on my head. Round and round it flew, never leaving me, as if wanting to play.*
>
> *I will try to be neither superstitious nor sentimental about this, but in the dark days after Nicholas's death I watched the regular visits of such a white bird as it hovered over the place where he died… It flew in tight circles, riding the thermals of a summer afternoon, then swooping towards me so close that often I ducked; then back it went to that tragic spot, soaring and diving, holding my attention with such a force that I have no idea how long I watched its antics. Then it was gone. I would have thought no more of it if it had not reappeared the next day, and the day after that.*[16] **❞**

Heiney goes on to describe how the visits of the bird became less frequent (or perhaps he noticed them less) as his acute grief subsided.

Bringing such human experiences and any accompanying beliefs into conversation with the Christian faith requires sensitivity and respect, and it can be challenging. Orthodox Christian teaching certainly does

[16] Heiney, P. (2015) One wild song: A voyage in a lost son's wake. (London: Bloomsbury). pp. 109-10.

not support the idea of the transmigration of spirits in any simple sense. In fact Christian teaching on life after death is difficult for most people to connect with at an intuitive level. It essentially states that immediately on death human beings go to a place of rest where they are in communion with the Godhead; their biological bodies decay, but they continue to exist; on the Last Day, when Christ appears in glory and heaven is married with earth, those who are in Christ rise with new eternal bodies; then there is some sort of judgment by Christ. It is very difficult to marry such bald dogmatic statements with personally compelling experiences like those of Heiney.

There is, however, more leverage in the area of images and poetry. The Bible is full of birds, including birds as metaphors for the human spirit and the divine Spirit. So at least some points of connection can be identified and resonances drawn out. For example:

> *O that I had wings like a dove! I would fly away and be at rest; truly, I would flee far away; I would lodge in the wilderness; I would hurry to find a shelter for myself from the raging wind and tempest.*
> **Psalm 55:6-8**

> *How lovely is your dwelling place, O LORD of hosts! My soul longs, indeed it faints for the courts of the LORD; my heart and my flesh sing for joy to the living God. Even the sparrow finds a home, and the swallow a nest for herself, where she may lay her young, at your altars, O LORD of hosts, my King and my God.*

Happy are those who live in your house, ever singing your praise. 🙙
Psalm 84:1-4

🙖 *In those days Jesus came from Nazareth of Galilee and was baptised by John in the Jordan. And just as he was coming up out of the water, he saw the heavens torn apart and the Spirit descending like a dove on him. And a voice came from heaven, "You are my Son, the Beloved; with you I am well pleased."* 🙙
Mark 1:9-11

🙖 *[Jesus] also said, "With what can we compare the kingdom of God, or what parable will we use for it? It is like a mustard seed, which, when sown upon the ground, is the smallest of all the seeds on earth; yet when it is sown it grows up and becomes the greatest of all shrubs, and puts forth large branches, so that the birds of the air can make nests in its shade."* 🙙

Mark 4: 30-2

Along with texts such as these, the traditional Christian iconography of angels is also very important here. Angels are (winged) heavenly messengers who come into their own at points where heaven touches earth, and who offer a natural bridge between folk spirituality and the Christian Gospel. It's not uncommon for a prematurely deceased individual to be idealised and asserted to be an angel. While this idea is, again, at odds with orthodox Christian teaching, it's a serious attempt to make sense of loss and manage grief, and should be worked with sensitively; the underlying instinct that the deceased has achieved fulfilment through profound transformation is sound and can be affirmed.

This brief indicative example is focused on birds and other winged creatures. Hopefully, you will be able to develop it further and also do something similar in relation to some of the other common human ideas and images for death.

Some answers to some FAQs

One cannot anticipate every question asked or issue raised in this session, but here are some suggestions for engaging with some of the more frequent and difficult ones:

Will I see my loved ones again in the next life?

While Jesus' words about the resurrection indicate that things will be profoundly different (Matthew 22:29-30), he does not say that we will be separated from our loved ones. St Paul says that 'we will be together with them' (1 Thessalonians 4:17) at Christ's second coming, precisely because he does not want his readers to 'grieve as others do who have no hope' (v.13). It may be helpful to tell a widow(er) that the marriage service words 'till death us do part' were probably originally 'till death us depart', and do not signify a final separation.

Am I/was my loved one good enough to face my maker just as we are?

This worry lies behind the resurgence of interest in the mediaeval notion of purgatory or related ideas about a process of continuing self-improvement after death, neither of which have biblical support. It may be helpful to stress the idea of 'faith not works' to Christians who are familiar with this idea. More broadly, the emphasis of the gospel is on God's seeking out those who are lost more than their finding their way to him (Luke 19:10); Luke 15 offers a really helpful way of exploring this. The incident of the thief on the cross (Luke 23:42-43) tells us that at the end of life the most unlikely people can do private business with God of which we are unaware. This may be a great comfort to those who have been praying for a change of heart in a loved one with little obvious effect.

My loved one died by suicide – where is s/he?

There is an ancient Christian tradition that in the darkness of Holy Saturday Jesus descended to preach to the 'spirits in prison' (1 Peter 3:19; see also Matthew 12:40; Ephesians 4:9). It is referred to in the Apostles' Creed and was the basis of the mediaeval idea of the 'harrowing of hell'. Whatever we make of this, it opens up the vitally important notion that there is nowhere so dark and wretched that it is beyond the redeeming reach of God in Christ. Here is a link to a rather cheerful depiction of this which you may like to use: eastdailyoffice.files.wordpress.com/2015/04/holysaturday-harrowingofhell-english-c1240.jpg

Is there a hell and, if so, who goes there?

There's no getting away from the fact that Jesus talked about hell in very vivid terms. However, his words are always in the context of God's ultimate judgment of those in power who have exploited or neglected the weak (Matthew 18:23-35; Luke 16:19-31, Mark 9: 42-48). It is all about God's justice. The parable of the wheat and the tares (Matthew 13:24-30) tells us that we cannot know what the final reckoning will involve other than that it will be fair, and so it's not good for us to judge or speculate. What we do know is that Christ will recognise his own, and that this will include 'other sheep that do not belong to this fold' (John 10:16). You may find it helpful to refer participants to CS Lewis' 'The last battle' if they wish to explore this further.

What about stillborn babies and late miscarriages?

Jesus said 'Let the little children come to me; do not stop them; for it is to such as these that the kingdom of God belongs.' (Mark 10:13). He did not qualify this statement with a demand for baptism. The New Testament is clear: infants have a special place in the heart of God.

Is it OK to pray for deceased loved ones?

This question is more likely to come from people from a protestant background who may have been brought up to believe that praying for the dead is like the mediaeval practice saying masses for the dead to get them through purgatory quicker, yet find that they have a great desire to pray for those they love and see no more. It may be helpful to explain that intercession is turning to God with people on our heart and, as our loved ones do not cease to exist at death, it makes sense to pray for them too. If we believe that they are already in some sort of communion with God we can also pray **with** them as part of the 'Communion of Saints.' Within the Eucharist the Sanctus – 'with angels and archangels, and with all the company of heaven,' – can become a focus for this, as can All Saints' Day.

Why didn't God heal my loved-one(s) even though I prayed faithfully?

It is both good and natural to pray for the physical cure of someone we love but at some point prayers may need to shift towards praying for a good death. This is part of letting go and acknowledges that death is the earthly destination for us all. After all, every person who was healed in the Bible died eventually (even Lazarus). A helpful short reflection can be found here: _www.christianitytoday.com/biblestudies/bible-answers/ theology/playingfavorites.html_

Conclusion

15 MINS

This session is the most open of all, yet it comes at the end of the course and so attention must be paid to good closure. Draw the discussion to a close and, if you have used the reflection cards, consider asking individual participants to read out the texts. Even if you don't do this, make sure that you finish by reading this extract from Revelation:

> 66 *God himself will be with them; he will wipe every tear from their eyes. Death will be no more; mourning and crying and pain will be no more, for the first things have passed away.* 99
> **Revelation 21: 1-4**

Finish the course with your usual prayer, if appropriate. You may wish to add a final farewell by using the words of the Grace (2 Corinthians 13:13). If you are in a more 'catholic' setting it may be good to end with 'May the souls of the faithful departed, through the mercy of God, rest in peace.' To which the response is, 'and rise in glory.'

During the post-session period while refreshments are being shared, it is a good idea to ask participants to complete a simple evaluation form. Go to page 73 to find the web page from which a form can be downloaded.

Further resources

ON THE WEBSITE

Please go to our website **www.deathlife.org.uk** to find further information.

Go to **www.deathlife.org.uk/course/** to download:

- Death attitude questionnaire (preparatory exercise)
- Flyer
- Evaluation form

Go to **www.deathlife.org.uk/good-practice/help/** to find organisations that can provide support.

FROM THE STORE

To buy reflection cards for use in Session 6 go to: **https://store.oxford. anglican.org/products/deathlife-cards/**

To buy further copies of this handbook go to: **https://store.oxford. anglican.org/products/deathlife-handbook/**

SOME SELECTED BACKGROUND READING

Albans, K. & Johnson, M. (2013). *God, me and being very old: stories of spirituality in later life.* London: SCM Press.

Badham, P. (2013). *Making sense of death and immortality*. London: SPCK.

Brayne, S. (2010). *The D word: Talking about dying.* London: Continuum.

Carter, M. (2014). *Dying to live: A theological and practical workbook on death, dying and bereavement.* London: SCM.

Davies, D. (1997). *Death, ritual and belief.* London: Cassell.

Davies, D. (2007). *The theology of death.* London: Bloomsbury.

Frankl, V. (2004). *Man's search for meaning.* London: Rider, new edition (but several editions available).

Gawande, A. (2014). *Being mortal: Illness, medicine and what matters at the end.* London: Profile Books.

Gibson, F. (2011). *Reminiscence and life story work: A practical guide.* London: Jessica Kingsley.

Giddings, P., Down, M., Sugden, E., & Tuckwell,G. (2017). *Talking about dying: Help in facing death and dying.* London: Wilberforce.

Gooder, P. (2011). Heaven. London: SPCK.

Kalinithi, P. (2017). *When breath becomes air: What makes life living in the face of death.* London: Penguin.

Kastenbaum (2000). *The psychology of death.* London: Free Association.

Kastenbaum, R. (2004). *On our way: The final passage through life and death.* University of California Press.

Kellehear, A. (2007). *A social history of dying.* Cambridge: Cambridge University Press.

Lampard, J. (2015). *Go forth, Christian Soul: The biography of a prayer.* Eugene, OR: Wipf & Stock.

MacKinlay, E. (2006). *Aging, spirituality and palliative care.* Binghamton, NY: Haworth Press.

Mannix, L. (2017). *With the end in mind: Dying, death and wisdom in an age of denial.* London: Collins.

Neale, R. (1971). *The art of dying.* New York: Harper & Rowe.

Rose, J. & Paterson, M. (2013). *Enriching ministry: Pastoral supervision in practice.* London: SCM.

Taylor, J. (2012). *Holy dying.* London: Forgotten books, classic edition (but several editions available).

The Archbishops' Council (2015). *Grave Talk: Cards and Facilitator's Guide.* London: Church House Publishing.

Thompson, B. & Neimeyer, R. (2014). *Grief and the expressive arts: practices for creating meaning.* New York: Routledge.

Vanstone, W.H. (2006). *The stature of waiting.* Harrisburg, PA: Moorehouse.

Wharton, B. (2015). *Voices from the hospice: Staying with life through suffering and waiting.* London: SCM.

Winter, D. (2013). *At the end of the day: Enjoying life in the departure lounge.* Oxford: BRF.

Woodward, J. (2005). *Befriending death.* London: SPCK.

Wright, N.T. (2011). *Surprised by hope.* London: SPCK.

And some useful listening:

BBC Radio 4 'We need to talk about death' introduced by Joan Bakewell: **bbc.co.uk/programmes/b09kgksn/episodes/downloads**

About the author

Joanna Collicutt is Adviser for Spiritual Care for Older People (SCOP) for the Anglican diocese of Oxford. She combines this post with a lectureship at Ripon College Cuddesdon (a centre training people for ministry in the Church of England). She is also an associate priest in an Oxfordshire parish.

After early experience in nursing, Joanna practised for many years as a clinical psychologist, initially working in the area of adult mental health before moving into neurology, neurosurgery, and neurological rehabilitation, finally becoming head of Psychological Services at the Nuffield Orthopaedic NHS Trust in Oxford. Her PhD was on anxiety states following brain injury, and she has a continuing interest in the psychological processing of trauma.

After a career break to study theology at Wycliffe Hall, Joanna began to research the interface between psychology and Christian faith, a longstanding passion. From 2006-2011 she was director of the MA programme in Psychology of Religion at Heythrop College, University of London, where she also taught undergraduate psychology modules in neuroscience and positive psychology, before moving back to Oxford to take up her present posts. More recently she has completed an MA in Christianity and the arts at King's College London.

In addition to many research papers and several book chapters, Joanna has written or co-written ten books. These include *Ethical practice in brain injury rehabilitation* (OUP, 2007); *The Dawkins Delusion?* (SPCK: 2007); *Jesus and the Gospel women* (SPCK, 2009); *The psychology of Christian character formation* (SCM, 2015); *Being mindful, being Christian* (Lion-Hudson, 2016); *Thinking of you: A theological and resource for the spiritual care of people with dementia* (BRF, 2017).

She enjoys making and listening to music, gardening, visiting art galleries, and family life.